Historic England

England's Redundant Post-War Coal- and Oil-Fired Power Stations

Guidelines for Recording and Archiving Their Records

Summary

This guidance note, published by Historic England – the Government's adviser on the historic environment – provides advice to the Energy Industry on the appropriate and proportionate level of recording of redundant power plants for posterity. The guidance covers description, investigation, photographic and videographic recording of the structures; approaches to oral history and information-gathering from the workers on the site and the local community, and advice on archiving the historic records and artefacts.

This guidance was written by Jonathan Clarke.
Edited by Susie Barson, Wayne Cocroft and Paul Backhouse.

Published by Historic England February 2016.
All images © Historic England unless otherwise stated.

HistoricEngland.org.uk/advice/...

Front cover
Ironbridge B power station, Shropshire.
Cooling towers at night.

Contents

Image above
Kingsnorth power station, Medway.
Interior of control room.

Introduction

Coal- and oil-fired power stations are among the largest and most recognisable industrial complexes the 20th century produced. They had a profound impact on the British landscape, visually, environmentally, and culturally, and the electricity they generated had a transformational impact on our economy and society. Reaching an unrivalled scale and level of technological sophistication by the 1960s, these enormous installations – the 'great temples to the carbon age'* – are fast reaching the end of their useful lives. *Neil Cossons, *Conservation Bulletin* 65, Winter 2010: Inherited Infrastructure: 6.

Historic England as the Government's principal adviser on the historic environment, has been considering the extent to which post-war coal- and oil-fired power stations have historic and architectural interest. When assessing for listing, particularly careful selection is required for buildings from the period after 1945, and at this time protection of these power stations by listing, and of any associated designed landscaped by registration, is very unlikely. A number of Certificates of Immunity from Listing (COIs) have already been issued. Further advice on listing can be found in 'Utilities and Communications Structures: a guide to outline the selection criteria used when listing utilities and communications structures' (April 2011).

Historic England recognises the important role these power stations played in meeting the nation's energy needs during the twentieth century, their high technological interest and wider landscape impact. We have commissioned a number of reports (Clark 2015a) and a summary overview on 20th –century coal- and oil-fired power stations is available on-line in the Historic England in the 'Introduction to Heritage Assets' series (Clark 2015b).

To complement this initial work further records are needed, especially of those power stations that have closed or are facing closure. Such records should be undertaken to an appropriate and proportionate level that is necessary to understand the history, operation and development of these sites. Such an approach is in line with the policies set out in the National Planning Policy Framework (DCLG 2012) and, in particular chapter 12, paragraph 141, where developers are required: 'to record and advance understanding of the significance of any heritage assets to be lost (wholly or in part) in a manner proportionate to their importance and the impact, and to make this evidence (and any archive generated) publicly accessible'.

Although this guidance specifically refers to **post-war coal- and oil-fired power stations** it outlines a methodological approach which can be applied to other types of large scale 20th-century industrial heritage assets and infrastructure that are being or about to be decommissioned.

1 Recording and Archiving Guidelines

1.1 Overview

There are three strands to this historic environment exercise, designed to collectively unlock the rich store of information contained in these enormous installations and to safeguard their most significant records and artefacts:

1. The creation and compilation of an investigative record for each power station site, based on the description, analysis and interpretation of evidence embodied in the buildings, structures and designed and working landscape and in a range of documentary sources.

This will consist of a number of interrelated activities and products:

- Investigation

- Photographic recording

- Videographic recording (where appropriate)

- A synthetic report

2. The creation of an oral history archive, based on the oral testimony of a range of personnel who served in these installations

3. The selection and deposition within local or national repositories of historic documents and artefacts

These three mutually reinforcing elements form the basis of a method of capturing and studying key evidence, material and intangible, of the remains of England's surviving post-war fossil-fuelled power stations, and of conveying the historical, technological, social, and architectural understanding and significance of each site. They also make allowance for the selection and deposition of significant documents and artefacts produced for, or during the life of the works, such that they can be conserved and publicly accessed within local and institutional archives and local, independent or national museums.

2 Recording of Power Stations and Their Landscaped Settings

2.1 Investigation

The principal aim for the recording of any coal- and oil-fired installation should initially be to gain a high level overview of the facility in its landscape. Such an approach will enable broad functional areas to be identified and illustrate the relationships and linkages between the different areas, many of which may have altered through time as activities have changed. From this preliminary analysis it should be possible to identify groups of buildings, individual structures or structural elements, plant and machinery, and landscape features that are worthy of more detailed documentation.

Power stations created their own distinctive industrial landscapes, through coal and fuel oil transmission, ash and dust disposal, road and rail access systems and so forth. Additionally, landscape architecture became a key aspect of the Central Electricity Generating Board's (CEGB) policy from its formation in 1958, with leading specialist architects brought it to ameliorate, or help harmonise the sites' built components. An analytical understanding of the layout of the buildings, and the functional relationship between them and the landscaped environment they both inhabit and created is a fundamental objective.

Figure 1
Fawley power station, Hampshire. Exterior of turbine hall.

Figure 2
Grain power station, Medway.

This information will probably be most intelligibly gathered and collated by annotating large-scale plans, maps and diagrams of the site. These records can be subsequently re-presented to depict, in intelligible form, the phased development of the site and the functional areas within it. Diagrams interpreting the movement of materials and production of energy (process flow), or the segregation of activities (eg, permeability diagrams) might be warranted, so long as these are not unduly technical in nature, and the evidence supporting the interpretations is provided. Such graphical exercises should be relatively straightforward since the vast majority of the buildings will have been used for a single function throughout their working lives, and diagrams are often contained in brochures that marked the opening of the facility.

2.2 Photographic recording

The size and complexity of these sites favours photography as a more efficient way of capturing data than either drawings derived from accurate measured survey or written description. As noted above, Historic England aerial photographic recording is ongoing, so only ground-based photography is required, to supplement that being undertaken by Historic England. The aim should be to photograph before closure, to record how spaces and plant are being used.

Photography should be used to document the exterior appearance of the site from a variety of viewpoints, and, within the site itself, to document the buildings/structural components in relation to one another, and to the landscaped environs.

Figure 3 (top)
Kingsnorth power station, Medway.
Exterior of turbine hall and boiler house

Figure 4 (above)
Kingsnorth power station, Medway.
Interior of control room.

For efficiency and coverage, oblique three-quarter views of individual buildings rather than systematic recording of external elevations are to be preferred. However, discretion is required: where, for instance, an individual elevation embodies an unusual degree of engineering or architectural input, views at right angles to the plane of the elevation may also be appropriate. The oblique three-quarter view preference is also applicable – with similar caveat – to the interiors of the (accessible) buildings, structures and circulation areas. Where a high vantage point is available, this should be utilised to permit longer, more revealing views of the floor space. It is important that at least some general views of interiors convey a sense of scale, through for example inclusion of a person or familiar object.

Figures 5 (top) and 6 (above)
Kingsnorth power station, Medway.
Details of plant to boiler house.

Any external or internal detail, structural or decorative, which is relevant to the building's design, development or use and which does not show adequately on general views, should merit additional coverage. General, and selective details of major machinery and plant is essential, covering all processes within the main complex: steam-raising plant (boiler layout, flues, draught plant, pulverised fuel equipment, ash-and dust-handling plant etc), turbo-generators, condensing and feed-heating plant; main steam and reheat piping, water treatment and chlorination plant and so forth. Control rooms might be recorded with panoramic images, close attention should be paid to the ergonomics of their design and the eye-line views of the operators.

Attention should also be paid to the visual character and architectural treatment of the buildings and structures: colour, texture and finish were not always limited the administrative or welfare buildings, but sometimes extended to cooling towers, switch houses, chimneys etc. Photographic views should accordingly be framed to illustrated the original design intentions of the consultant architects for the power station, deduced either from documentary sources or inferred from the grouping and massing of the buildings and their setting. The social history embodied in the interior of welfare facilities such as canteens is also worthy of record.

The preferred format for digital images is unsharpened Adobe RGB 8 bit tiffs.

Figure 7
Grain power station, Medway.
Detail of dismantled turbine.

7

2.3 Videographic recording

As a supplement to photography, and not as an alternative, videographic recording should be considered for those power stations still with active processes. This might include observable movement within the turbine/boiler house, fuel delivery systems (including 'merry-go-round railways'), ash disposal conveyors, 'smoking' flues, stacks and cooling towers, control room display boards. An aspiration might be to record workers describing the operation they are engaged in; for example operatives at control desks explaining how the panels are arranged and what functions they relate to.

High resolution digital video as means of recording dynamic industrial processes has gained increasing recognition in recent years, and as a medium it offers exciting possibilities for capturing social as well as technological history:

> 'The major challenge that faces the archaeology of the industrial period in future years is the need to move beyond the documentation of machines and the history of technology, to create stories that highlight the individual and collective social experience of industrial worlds that are now fading, but which still cast a long shadow over our post-industrial lives'.

E. Casella and J Symonds, Eds 2005
Industrial Archaeology: Future Directions,
p. 53.

2.4 Synthetic report

Insights and understanding derived from investigation, photography and *in situ* historic records should be presented in an analytical report that is concise yet well-illustrated. Photographs on their own present evidence but seldom convey understanding, so this written account is extremely important as an overall synthesis of the historical, architectural and technological inquiry. Its emphasis will be on analysis and interpretation as well as description, and, wherever possible, drawing out the particularities and significances of the site. As well as being illustrated by new and (if locally available) historic photographs, it will incorporate plans and diagrams showing the phased development of the site, the functional areas within it, the movement of materials and the production of energy. A descriptive list of photographs, including view's orientation (and GPS coordinates, if images are 'Geotagged') and the date taken, and cross-referenced to its digital file, should be appended to the report. A descriptive list of documents and artefacts consulted, encountered, and deposited (together with the name(s) of the receiving archive) in the course of the project should also be appended.

3 Historic Records and Artefacts
Archival and Curatorial Procedures

3.1 Historic records

The closure of any power station is likely to lead to the identification of records relating to the design, construction, development and operation of the station, which the relevant power generating company does not need to retain as part of its own documentation strategy.

The post-war power station programme is currently not well documented within publicly accessible archives. As a result such material is potentially of interest to several archival repositories who are concerned to document the operation of these major undertakings from both a local and national context. Within England these repositories may include:

- The relevant local authority record office. Such repositories are likely to be particularly interested in the role the site has played in supporting and shaping local communities and economies

- The Historic England Archive. This is a national archive of the historic environment, and its primary interest is in historic material on the design, construction and operation of the site which can sit alongside any new record which is being created

- Specialist repositories such as the Archive of the Institution of Engineering and Technology

Themes and types of record which are likely to be of interest will include:

- Material on the design and construction of the site, and in particular anything which casts light on the design process, such as copies of architects' original design drawings. This may include photographs, reports, and plans and drawings

- Material relating to landscaping design and to any associated public art or decorative elements

- Documentation of major changes or developments to the site, such as the creation of new generating capacity

- Records relating to the 'public face' of the station including for example publicity brochures, videos, press cuttings or papers relating to local committees or initiatives

- Material which succinctly describes the operation of the site, particularly in terms of showing how the various processes worked and fitted together

- The working life of staff at the station

- All formats of material are potentially relevant, including photographic prints and negatives, drawings and plans (including electronic files), files, reports, films and videos etc

Material which is likely to require more stringent selection will include:

- Detailed technical documentation of plant and building elements

- Records of routine operation and maintenance

3.2 Historic artefacts

Objects and equipment relating to the operation and maintenance of the station are likely to survive in many post-war power stations. As material evidence of the electricity supply industry, they are of significance to British local and national life, and the technology of the 20th century.

Machinery and objects from post-war power stations are underrepresented within publicly accessible museums, both local and specialised. Therefore such material is potentially of interest to a number of museums which are concerned with collecting, safeguarding and making accessible artefacts relating to the electricity supply industry.

Figure 8
Ironbridge B power station, Shropshire.
Interior of cooling tower.

Within England these repositories will include:

- The relevant local authority museum. Since these generally house collections that reflect local history and heritage, objects associated or illustrative of the site's social and cultural life, and its impact on the local economy are more likely to meet with established acquisitions policies than objects of purely technological interest Independent museums specialising in industrial or technological history

- National museums holding collections considered to be of national importance. The Science Museum, which already holds the national collections in science, medicine, technology and engineering should be considered if the object is of exemplary technological or engineering value. The Museum of Science and Technology in Manchester has an extensive electricity collection. However, it should be noted that museums' collection policy is governed by narratives (rather than gap-filling), and its broad direction is shaped by key themes that are periodically reviewed

Themes and types of object which are likely to be of possible interest will include:

- A small yet meaningful part of the site's technology, such a rotor blade from one of the innovatory 500MW turbo-alternators or a component from one of the 400kv substation's transformers

- Architectural site and training models

- A small yet meaningful constituent of the site's architecture or interior design, such as a display/control panel from the control room, murals, artwork and sculpture

- Architectural or technological models, depicting the site's components and its operation

- CEGB-issue work-wear, safety equipment or inspection/maintenance tools

- Memorabilia associated with the welfare and social life of the employees, such as club trophies, medals, canteen tableware etc

Material which is likely to be of less interest will include:

- Objects which are unduly large, heavy or commonplace, or the significance of which is lost in an *ex-situ* context

If accepted by a museum, objects will be accessioned and the ownership will be transferred to the museum permanently.

4 Oral History Recording

As a means of creating a permanent record that contributes to an understanding of the past worlds of 20th-century power stations, the oral testimony of personnel who served in these installations is invaluable. Whilst many of the personnel from the early years of the CEGB are deceased, many, occupying key roles and whose recollections are important to understanding the operation of the works will still be connected to individual sites, or at least be traceable. These people will not only be able to recount for posterity much of their own knowledge and experiences, but provide a perspective on what it was like to work with the CEGB, and even the privatised organisations that came after it. Their testimony is particularly important. But capturing the experiences of more recent entrants whose experiences are solely that of the privatised electricity supply industry is also of significance, since the UK experience of privatisation has been highly influential globally. There is considerable scope here for intercommunication or coaction with the *National Life Stories Project: Oral History of the Electricity Supply Industry in the UK*. Whilst this project, based within the British Library, included interviews with some power station workers, its breadth and scope (drawing interviewees whose careers spanned over each of the key areas of policy, technology, operations and organisations) precluded full representation of the power generation sector. Thus there is considerable scope to capture the recollections and experiences of a range of employees who worked, or still work, at those post-war power stations that are of concern here.

See http://www.bl.uk/reshelp/findhelprestype/ sound/ohist/ohnls/electricityindustry/ electricityindustry.html

It is highly recommended that heritage consultants conduct interviews with willing current and former employees, and/or members of the local community.

The capture of the oral record should be submitted to an appropriate archive.

Figure 9
Kingsnorth power station, Medway.
General view of coal hopper.

5 Where to Get Advice

Wayne Cocroft, Senior Investigator, Research Group, will be able to provide advice on the recording and archiving of the Redundant Post-War Coal and Oil-Fired Power Stations. Wayne will also be able to indicate contacts and support for the undertaking of aerial survey, photography and archive solutions and advice available through Historic England.

He can be contacted via wayne.cocroft@HistoricEngland.org.uk or through the East of England office:
Brooklands
24 Brooklands Avenue
Cambridge CB2 8BU
Tel: 01223 582749

Figure 10
Grain power station, Medway.
Interior of turbine hall in process of being decommissioned.

6 Bibliography

Brown, D.H. *Archaeological Archives: A guide to best practice in creation, compilation, transfer and curation*. Institute of Field Archaeologists on behalf of the Archaeological Archives Forum http://www.archaeologyuk.org/archives/Archives_Best_Practice.pdf

Clarke, J 2015a 'High Merit': existing post-war coal and oil-fired power stations in context', [includes a bibliography of individual power stations]. Typescript report.

Clarke, J 2015b *20th-Century Coal and Oil-Fired Electric Power Generation* Historic England Introduction to Heritage Assets https://HistoricEngland.org.uk/images-books/publications/iha-20thcentury-coal-oil-fired-electric-power-generation/

Cossons, N 2010 'Historic infrastructure', in English Heritage 2010, 4-7.

DCLG (Department for Communities and Local Government) 2012: *National Planning Policy Framework* https://www.gov.uk/government/publications/national-planning-policy-framework-2

DCMS (Department of Culture, Media and Sport) 2010 *Principles of Selection for Listing Buildings* (March 2010) https://www.gov.uk/government/publications/principles-of-selection-for-listing-buildings

English Heritage 2006 *Understanding historic buildings a guide to good recording practice* English Heritage: Swindon https://HistoricEngland.org.uk/images-books/publications/understanding-historic-buildings/

English Heritage 2007 *Understanding the archaeology of landscapes A guide to good recording practice* English Heritage: Swindon https://HistoricEngland.org.uk/images-books/publications/understanding-archaeology-of-landscapes/

English Heritage 2010 *The disposal of historic assets: guidance for government departments and non-departmental public bodies* English Heritage OGC DCMS https://www.HistoricEngland.org.uk/images-books/publications/disposal-heritage-assets/

English Heritage 2010 Inherited Infrastructure *Conservation Bulletin* **65** https://HistoricEngland.org.uk/images-books/publications/conservation-bulletin-65/

English Heritage 2011 *Designation Listing Selection Guide: Utilities and Communications Structures: a guide to outline the selection criteria used when designating utilities and communication structures.* English Heritage: https://HistoricEngland.org.uk/images-books/publications/dlsg-utilities-communication-structures/

English Heritage 2011 'Saving the Age of Industry', *Conservation Bulletin* **67** (Autumn 2011).https://HistoricEngland.org.uk/images-books/publications/conservation-bulletin-67/

Horrocks S and Lean 2011 T 'NLS Scoping Study: An Oral History of The Electricity Supply Industry' English Heritage National Life Stories, November 2011. http://www.bl.uk/reshelp/findhelprestype/sound/ohist/ohnls/electricityindustry/nls_electricityindustryscopingstudy.pdf

Contemporary periodicals such as the *Electrical Review, Electrical Times* and the *Engineering and Boiler House Review* are good sources for articles relating to the construction and commissioning of power plants.

Figure 11
Ironbridge B power station, Shropshire.
Base of Cooling tower.

Contact Historic England

East Midlands
2nd Floor, Windsor House
Cliftonville
Northampton NN1 5BE
Tel: 01604 735460
Email: eastmidlands@HistoricEngland.org.uk

East of England
Brooklands
24 Brooklands Avenue
Cambridge CB2 8BU
Tel: 01223 582749
Email: eastofengland@HistoricEngland.org.uk

Fort Cumberland
Fort Cumberland Road
Eastney
Portsmouth PO4 9LD
Tel: 023 9285 6704
Email: fort.cumberland@HistoricEngland.org.uk

London
1 Waterhouse Square
138-142 Holborn
London EC1N 2ST
Tel: 020 7973 3700
Email: london@HistoricEngland.org.uk

North East
Bessie Surtees House
41-44 Sandhill
Newcastle Upon Tyne
NE1 3JF
Tel: 0191 269 1255
Email: northeast@HistoricEngland.org.uk

North West
3rd Floor, Canada House
3 Chepstow Street
Manchester M1 5FW
Tel: 0161 242 1406
Email: northwest@HistoricEngland.org.uk

South East
Eastgate Court
195-205 High Street
Guildford GU1 3EH
Tel: 01483 252020
Email: southeast@HistoricEngland.org.uk

South West
29 Queen Square
Bristol BS1 4ND
Tel: 0117 975 1308
Email: southwest@HistoricEngland.org.uk

Swindon
The Engine House
Fire Fly Avenue
Swindon SN2 2EH
Tel: 01793 445050
Email: swindon@HistoricEngland.org.uk

West Midlands
The Axis
10 Holliday Street
Birmingham B1 1TG
Tel: 0121 625 6870
Email: westmidlands@HistoricEngland.org.uk

Yorkshire
37 Tanner Row
York YO1 6WP
Tel: 01904 601948
Email: yorkshire@HistoricEngland.org.uk

We are the public body that looks after
England's historic environment. We champion
historic places, helping people understand,
value and care for them.

Please contact
guidance@HistoricEngland.org.uk
with any questions about this document.

HistoricEngland.org.uk

If you would like this document in a different
format, please contact our customer services
department on:

Tel: 0370 333 0607
Fax: 01793 414926
Textphone: 0800 015 0174
Email: customers@HistoricEngland.org.uk

HEAG088
Publication date: February 2016 © Historic England
Design: Historic England

Printed in Great Britain
by Amazon

84339569R00016